ESSENTIAL LIBRARY OF AMERICAN WARS

# REVOLUTIONARY WAR

ABDO
Publishing Company

# REVOLUTIONARY WAR

BY ROBERT GRAYSON

CONTENT CONSULTANT
Robert J. Allison, Chair, History Department
Suffolk University

# CREDITS



Printed in the United States of America,
North Mankato, Minnesota
052013
112013

THIS BOOK CONTAINS AT LEAST 10% RECYCLED MATERIALS.

Editor: Lauren Coss
Series Designer: Emily Love

**Photo Credits**

Domenick D'Andrea/National Guard Image Gallery, cover, 2, 37; North Wind/North Wind Picture Archives, 6, 11, 17, 28, 35, 38, 47, 48, 58, 62, 66, 71, 74, 76, 85, 88, 91, 93, 98 (left), 99 (left), 99 (right), 101 (right); Jackson Walker/National Guard Image Gallery, 18; Library of Congress, 23; J. Fielding/Library of Congress, 24, 101 (left); Keith Reicher/iStockphoto, 26; Ken Riley/National Guard Image Gallery, 42, 98 (right); Interim Archives/Getty Images, 50; The Werner Company/Library of Congress, 57; Hulton Archive/iStockphoto, 61; Stock Montage/Getty Images, 65; Thinkstock, 81; Red Line Editorial, 87, 100, 101; U.S. National Archives and Records Administration, 97

Library of Congress Control Number: 2013932669

**Cataloging-in-Publication Data**

Grayson, Robert.
Revolutionary War / Robert Grayson.
p. cm. -- (Essential library of American wars)
Includes bibliographical references and index.
ISBN 978-1-61783-879-8
1. United States--History--Revolution, 1775-1783--Juvenile literature. 2. Revolutionary War, 1775-1783--United States--Juvenile literature. I. Title.
973.3--dc23

2013932669

# CONTENTS

1

# A MUCH-NEEDED VICTORY

The Revolutionary War was not going well for the Americans in the summer of 1777. They had spent the last two years fighting for their independence from Great Britain, and they were losing. The British military's fighting force had many advantages over the Americans' Continental army. British King George III's troops, called redcoats because they wore scarlet woolen jackets, had entered the war well trained and heavily armed. By contrast, the Continental army, commanded by American general George Washington, was a ragtag group of fighters. Washington's men had little military experience and lesser-quality equipment than their British counterparts. Some members of local militias joined the Continental army.

In 1777, American military forces needed a victory that would alter the course of the Revolutionary War with the British in their favor.

The Americans relied on grit and courage, but most of the time, that had not been enough to win battles. American fighters, known as patriots, were often outnumbered and outgunned by the British army. The Americans lost battles they had started off winning. Death on the battlefield was taking a substantial toll on the American troops.

Great Britain controlled New York City and much of the surrounding area and all of eastern Canada. The British Royal Navy was in a strong position, ready to attack anywhere along the Eastern Seaboard. British military commanders felt the king's army was just one crushing victory away from ending the American uprising altogether.

## A PLAN TO CRUSH THE REVOLT

Washington's troops had won several battles in the difficult struggle. However, they had not been able to deliver a decisive blow. They needed to prove to possible allies they were up to the task of defeating Great Britain and winning the war. British military leaders were determined to win the war before that could happen. British general John Burgoyne hatched a plan he believed would force the Americans to surrender.

Burgoyne hoped to sever New England from the rest of the American colonies. Under the plan, Burgoyne would lead an army of 8,000 men southward from Quebec, Canada, to Albany, New York.[1] Half of Burgoyne's forces were British troops. The other half was made up of hired German soldiers, called Hessians, and Mohawk American Indians, who supported the British effort. Both groups would operate under Burgoyne's command.

A second British force, led by Colonel Barry St. Leger, would head east through the Mohawk Valley in upstate New York. At the same time, British general William Howe would lead troops north from New York City. The three forces would meet in Albany. There they could smash through the Continental army and gain control of the Hudson

## HESSIAN TROOPS

Great Britain needed additional manpower during the Revolutionary War, so it hired men from Germany to serve in the British army. Many of the hired soldiers came from the Hesse region of Germany and were known as Hessians. Approximately 30,000 Germans fought for the British in the American Revolution. More than 12,000 of these men were Hessians.[2]

River, isolating the four New England colonies from the other nine colonies.

The British saw the New England area, especially Boston, Massachusetts, as the base of operations for revolution supporters. Separating Boston and the rest of New England from the southern colonies would make it impossible for New England patriots to contribute soldiers and supplies to the revolutionary cause. Burgoyne believed this would break the Americans' spirit, ending the rebellion once and for all.

The plan started off well. Burgoyne's troops left Canada in June 1777. By early July, Burgoyne had won an easy victory in upstate New York, seizing Fort Ticonderoga, which had been held by the Americans. Before long, however, the British general's march toward Albany ran into trouble. The countryside was made up of swamps, gullies, and heavy underbrush. The rough terrain slowed Burgoyne's army.

The Continental army was familiar with the landscape. With the help of local militias, the army periodically attacked the British as they trekked through the marshy wilderness. The redcoats suffered losses each time they clashed with the American soldiers.

The American colonies at the time of the Revolutionary War

## SETBACKS FOR THE BRITISH

By August, Burgoyne's troops were running low on supplies because of the difficult conditions. He sent a detachment, or smaller group, to round up supplies. Lieutenant Colonel Friedrich Baum commanded the detachment. On August 16, patriot forces clashed with Baum's men in Walloomsac, New York, approximately ten miles (16 km) from Bennington, Vermont. In what became known as the Battle of Bennington, local militias from New Hampshire and Massachusetts killed or captured Baum's entire force, drastically reducing Burgoyne's manpower.

Colonel St. Leger had also faced a major setback earlier in August. On his way to join Burgoyne in Albany, St. Leger had attempted to capture Fort Stanwix. Fort Stanwix was a defensive stronghold for the Americans in the Mohawk River valley region of New York, which was populated by many of Great Britain's Mohawk allies. Initially, St. Leger's men fought the patriots for the fort. But the Continental army refused to give up its position. American reinforcements, led by General Benedict Arnold, held off the British attack.

When Arnold and his men arrived, Arnold spread out his troops. He tricked the British into thinking he was attacking with a larger force than he actually had. The misinformation scared off many of St. Leger's Mohawk allies, who fled. This convinced St. Leger to order his army to retreat, stopping the British advance to Albany through the Mohawk valley.

Meanwhile, in September, General Howe captured Philadelphia, Pennsylvania, the patriot's capital, before heading to Albany. He did not plan on the strong resistance he received from Washington's troops there. The Americans had to give up Philadelphia, but they delayed Howe. He and his men never made it to Albany. Burgoyne was left alone to carry out his plan to sever New England from the rest of

## TRAITOR

Benedict Arnold was one of the early supporters of independence from Great Britain. He fought bravely for the patriots in the war. He rose to the rank of general in the Continental army. After the British abandoned Philadelphia in June 1778, Arnold was named America's military commander of the city. However in 1780, Arnold began giving American military secrets to the British. He was exposed as a traitor in September and joined the British army, where he was made a general. He fought for the British during the rest of the Revolutionary War. After the war, he escaped to England with his family. In the United States today, his name is synonymous with being a traitor.

the colonies. Despite these setbacks, Burgoyne was committed to seeing his plan through.

## THE BATTLE OF SARATOGA

The Americans had been paying attention to the movement of the British troops, so they had a good idea of where the redcoats were going. On September 13, Burgoyne's men began crossing the Hudson River near Saratoga, New York, which was less than 40 miles (64 km) north of Albany. Patriot forces, led by General Horatio Gates, were ready for him.

The patriots had dug trenches into the rolling hills of an area known as Bemis Heights. On the morning of September 19, the Americans spotted the British army crossing through an abandoned farm approximately ten miles (16 km) south of Saratoga. The Battle of Saratoga was about to begin.

Gates's troops relentlessly fired on the enemy, stopping many of the redcoats. General Arnold, who had come down from the Mohawk valley to join the fight, led an American regiment that cut off advancing British troops in the middle of the farm. His soldiers inflicted heavy losses on the British, but by the end of the day, Burgoyne's troops had forced the Americans to fall back. The battle had taken a heavy toll on the

British, however. Burgoyne's troops suffered massive losses and were demoralized by the Americans' resolve. Furthermore, the patriots still blocked the road to Albany. The Continental army continued expanding as more troops arrived daily to join the battle.

### LONG SHOT

In the Battle of Saratoga, American snipers used American-made long rifles to pick off British troops. Long rifles were much more accurate than other guns used at the time. Long rifles were also light and slender compared to the cumbersome muskets of the day. Skilled marksmen could fire long rifles from a perch in a tree and hit a target more than 200 yards (183 m) away. British soldiers feared the long rifles.

Burgoyne hoped for reinforcements, but they never arrived. Skirmishes continued for days. Finally, on October 7, the British mounted another attack, which became known as the Battle of Bemis Heights, or the Second Battle of Saratoga. This time, the British were determined to force the Americans from Bemis Heights and gain access to the road to Albany. In the furious fighting that followed, the redcoats suffered heavy losses. By then, Burgoyne had lost more than 3,000 of his original 8,000 men.[3] He was surrounded by more than

20,000 American troops.[4] Burgoyne knew he would not be able to sustain his army in this position over the coming winter. Greatly outnumbered by the Americans, Burgoyne surrendered on October 17.

The Americans had their decisive victory. It would help convince France to support the colonies in their fight for independence. The win gave new hope to patriots in all the colonies. The Second Battle of Saratoga may have been a turning point in the Revolutionary War, but the war for independence was far from over.

Burgoyne's surrender to Gates following the Second Battle of Saratoga was an important victory for the Americans.

2

# COLONIAL UNREST

Before the Revolutionary War began in the spring of 1775, tensions had been building between Great Britain and its 13 American colonies for some time. The rift started shortly after the end of the French and Indian War (1754–1763), when Great Britain and American colonies fought against France and its American Indian allies.

The British and Americans eventually won the war, but the victory came at a steep price. The war had been very expensive, and it put a heavy strain on Great Britain's budget. The nation was already struggling with a soaring national debt due to costly wars with other European rivals. In addition, King George III now felt he needed to station British troops in North America. The king thought the colonies had to be

The French and Indian War was a costly war for the British government. It also increased tensions between American Indians and British colonists.

protected from the French settlers who remained in North America. He also feared attacks by American Indians, who may have been holding a grudge after the French and Indian War. Paying these North American troops added to Great Britain's money troubles, putting the country even further in debt. The king had a plan to lower his country's spiraling debt. He would tax the colonies.

## SOURCES OF CONFLICT

The colonists did not want British soldiers guarding the colonies, and they certainly did not want to pay for them. Most Americans viewed the British troops as an armed force that could be ordered to turn against the colonists at any time. Colonists were also frustrated by Great Britain's ban on westward expansion. After the French and Indian War, many Americans wanted to settle in the Ohio River valley on the western frontier beyond the Appalachian Mountains. But the British Parliament feared settlers' westward movement would spark costly conflicts between colonial settlers and the American Indians who had lived in the Ohio River valley for centuries. With the Proclamation of 1763, King George banned colonists from settling west of the Appalachians. The ban angered many colonists.

Then came a wave of unpopular taxes levied against the colonies by the British Parliament. One of the Parliament's most hated actions was its adoption of the Stamp Act in March 1765. The Stamp Act applied a sales tax to paper products used for legal documents, newspapers, pamphlets, and cards.

### NORTH AMERICA IN 1763

The treaty that ended the French and Indian War in 1763 left France with no territory in mainland North America. Great Britain got all of Canada, and as a result, Canada became a major staging area for British troops early in the American Revolution. Great Britain also ended up with nearly all North American territory east of the Mississippi River.

## COLONISTS FIGHT BACK

The Stamp Act sparked outrage throughout the colonies. Most colonists believed the British Parliament did not have the right to tax them. These colonists argued that since they did not elect anyone to Parliament, they were being taxed without representation. They saw this as a violation of British law. Colonists protested against the Stamp Act, making the slogan "no taxation without representation" the focus of their outrage.[1]

They threatened British agents who had been assigned to collect the tax.

Governing bodies in the colonies, known as assemblies, fought back as well. Virginia's colonial assembly passed a law stating it was the only governing body that could tax Virginians. Other colonial assemblies soon passed similar laws. In October 1765, representatives from nine of the colonies met in New York and issued a Declaration of Rights and Grievances. The document laid out the colonies' arguments against the taxes. It claimed Great Britain did not have the authority to tax the colonies because colonists were not represented in Parliament. It was the first time the colonies had banded together in a major joint action.

The tension between the British Parliament and the colonists only grew worse. Merchants in New York began boycotting British-made goods. The boycotts soon spread to Boston and Philadelphia. The British economy relied heavily on selling Great Britain's manufactured goods in the colonies, and the boycotts soon paid off. In March 1766, under pressure from the colonies, the Parliament repealed the Stamp Act. However, at the same time, it passed the Declaratory Act. This act declared Parliament had the legal authority to fully govern the

Colonists in Boston protested the Stamp Act.

colonies, including forcing them to pay taxes. Many colonists were outraged.

One year after passing the Declaratory Act, the British Parliament passed additional tax laws called the Townshend Acts. Under the Townshend Acts, imported goods from Great

King George III was king of Great Britain and Ireland from 1760 to 1820.

Britain were taxed, including glass, paint, cloth, paper, and tea. Protests erupted in the colonies almost immediately. These protests were even more vigorous than those over the Stamp Act. The colonies formed groups to organize and enforce boycotts against all British goods covered by the taxes. The boycotts were so effective that by 1770 Parliament repealed all taxes on British-imported goods except tea.

## BOSTON: THE HUB OF PROTEST

There was no place in colonial America where the protests against British taxes were as vocal and heated as Boston. Great Britain responded by sending troops to Boston to keep the peace. But sending soldiers only made the situation worse. Many Bostonians saw the soldiers' presence as a military occupation of their city.

Matters got even worse on March 5, 1770, when a mob of colonists attacked the British military barracks. The colonists were armed with rocks, clubs, and other weapons. When the colonists provoked the British soldiers, the soldiers fired on the crowd. When it was over, five colonists lay dead in the snowy street. Many other colonists were injured. Americans across the colonies were furious. Prominent Massachusetts political figures John Hancock and Samuel Adams led the colonial criticism of the shootings. Adams immediately labeled the confrontation the Boston Massacre.

Tempers flared once again in June 1772, when the British navy sent the *Gaspee* to patrol the Rhode Island coastline, looking for colonists who were smuggling goods into America without paying taxes on them. This did not sit well with the colonists. The citizens of Rhode Island did not want to pay

The Boston Massacre caused the rift between Great Britain and its American colonies to grow even wider.

taxes, and they felt the British had no right to patrol colonial waters. On the night of June 9, the *Gaspee* ran aground near Providence, Rhode Island. Colonists boarded the ship, subdued the crew, and burned the vessel. King George was furious about the incident. He ordered that those responsible for the attack be captured and brought to Great Britain for trial.

The thought of Americans being put on trial in Great Britain alarmed many colonists. Samuel Adams proposed the colonial assemblies establish committees of correspondence. This would allow colonial assemblies to communicate with one another, through letters, about the actions that should be taken against threats to American liberties.

### FATHER OF THE REVOLUTION

Samuel Adams was one of the earliest supporters of the Revolutionary War. Born in Boston, Adams came from a wealthy and politically active family. His second cousin, John Adams, would become the second president of the United States. Having failed in business as a young man, Samuel Adams turned to politics. As early as 1764, Adams opposed the British Parliament's plans to tax the colonies. He labeled the taxes a violation of colonial rights. Adams raised the point that the Parliament could not tax the colonies because the colonies had no representation in Parliament. He organized boycotts and demonstrations against the British taxes. He wrote letters to the other colonies, urging them to protest British taxation as well.

The American colonies were beginning to think about banding together to defend themselves against the British. But it would take one more incident, again in Boston, to incite the colonists to finally take up arms and fight for independence.

3

# SHOTS FIRED

In May 1773, the British Parliament passed the Tea Act. The act was designed to help the failing British East India Company, which had an excess of unsold tea. The act would allow the company to sell tea in the colonies at a lower cost while still paying the tax. This would create a monopoly on tea. Colonists were infuriated. The citizens of Boston demanded ships carrying tea from Great Britain to Boston Harbor be turned away. However, the governor of Massachusetts was determined to follow the law and pay the tax.

## MORE TROUBLES

In late 1773, three ships arrived in Boston Harbor carrying tea. They sat in the harbor with the tea still on board. The townspeople refused to unload the tea and pay the tax. On December 16, more than 100 colonists from Boston disguised themselves as American Indians. Then they boarded the ships

In December 1773, a group of colonists dressed as American Indians destroyed a shipment of British tea in an event known as the Boston Tea Party.

and dumped all the tea into the harbor. The British Parliament considered the incident, which became known as the Boston Tea Party, a deliberate act of defiance.

### BOILING POINT

Fifty-one women in Edenton, North Carolina, held a tea party of their own on October 25, 1774. Led by Penelope Barker, the protesters signed a declaration vowing they would not drink tea or use cloth imported from Great Britain. The group of protesters became known as the Edenton Tea Party. Barker said of the group: "Maybe it has only been men who have protested the king up to now. . . . That only means we women have taken too long to let our voices be heard. We are signing our names to a document, not hiding ourselves behind costumes like the men in Boston did at their tea party. The British will know who we are."[1]

King George was determined to punish Massachusetts, Boston in particular, for the Boston Tea Party. In March 1774, the British Parliament passed a series of laws known as the Coercive Acts to punish Massachusetts. One law suspended the Massachusetts government and banned town meetings. Another law closed Boston Harbor until colonists paid for the tea destroyed during the Boston Tea Party. The closure of the harbor hurt Boston's economy and eliminated many jobs.

The king replaced Massachusetts's governor with General Thomas Gage. Gage also served as the commander in chief of the British army in North America. One of Gage's first actions was to place Boston under martial law to crack down on rebellious protests.

The Coercive Acts only affected Massachusetts. King George had hoped this would isolate Massachusetts from the rest of the colonies. His plan backfired. The actions taken against Massachusetts only strengthened the other colonies' frustrations with the British Parliament. Representatives from the colonies formed a group called the Continental Congress. The delegates of the First Continental Congress met in Philadelphia in September 1774. Every colony except Georgia sent representatives to the Congress.

## THE COLONIES TAKE ACTION

The First Continental Congress passed a declaration of colonial rights, which upheld the colonies' right to govern themselves. The delegates also concluded that if British troops used force against any of the colonies, all the colonies should fight back as one. The Congress agreed to meet again in May 1775.

## GEORGIA'S ABSENCE

Georgia was the only colony not to send representatives to the First Continental Congress. Colonial leaders in Georgia were hoping Great Britain would send military troops to defend the colony from American Indians on its western frontier. They did not want to risk the British Parliament's anger. However, British aid never arrived. Georgia did not send delegates to the Second Continental Congress right away, but on July 8, 1775, Georgia decided to join the other colonies. Its delegates arrived in Philadelphia on July 20.

Shortly after the First Continental Congress ended, towns throughout the New England colonies started shoring up their defenses. Some civilians began stockpiling weapons and ammunition. These militiamen also began training in groups.

In March 1775, General Gage learned colonial militias had a substantial stash of weapons in Concord, Massachusetts, approximately 24 miles (39 km) west of Boston. Under orders from the British Parliament, Gage was preparing to confiscate the weapons being gathered in Concord. He was also determined to capture and imprison Hancock and Adams.

The citizens of Boston did not trust the British. They kept a close eye on the troops' every move. One patriot stumbled onto the British plan to go after the militias' weapons and tipped off the rest of the colonists. Boston silversmith Paul Revere and Doctor Joseph Warren, a leading Boston patriot, began watching the movement of British troops. On April 7, 1775, Revere and Warren gathered intelligence that Gage would be sending his men to raid Concord in approximately one week. Revere instructed the Concord militia to move its store of weapons. He also developed a series of signals to let the militias in towns on the way to Concord know when the British troops were heading their way and the path the troops were following.

## THE BRITISH ARRIVE

The British could have approached Concord from Boston by water, crossing the Charles River in boats, or by marching over land. If the British were coming by land, the patriots would hang a single lantern in Boston's Old North Church. If the British were coming by water, they would hang two lanterns. On the night of April 18, Gage ordered his troops to move out. They went by boat, and Revere's signal went out over the darkened countryside.

Revere and fellow patriot William Dawes mounted horses and rode out to warn colonists to be ready to battle the 700 armed redcoats heading toward Concord.[2] Most of the weapons had already been moved. However, Americans feared Gage's troops would capture Hancock and Adams. Both men were in Lexington, Massachusetts, approximately five miles (8 km) outside of Concord.

Revere and Dawes reached Lexington in plenty of time to warn of the impending British attack. Hancock and Adams escaped. Revere and Dawes met up with another rider, Samuel Prescott, and rode on to Concord. Meanwhile, militiamen in Lexington prepared for a fight. They hoped to stop, or at least slow, the British advance before the troops reached Concord.

As dawn broke on April 19, Gage's troops saw a line of 70 militiamen waiting for them in the middle of Lexington.[3] British commanders ordered the minutemen to leave. They refused. No one knows who fired the first shot, but chaos erupted as soon as it was fired. Eight militiamen were killed, and nine were wounded. After the skirmish, the British moved on. Only one redcoat had been slightly injured.

The British soon reached Concord, where approximately 250 militiamen were ready for a fight. But instead of attacking

When Revere spotted two lanterns in the Old North Church, he knew British soldiers would be traveling by water.

right away, the colonists fell back to the North Bridge, approximately one mile (1.6 km) outside of town. The redcoats split up, sending regiments throughout Concord to search buildings for weapons. This gave the Concord militia time to wait for reinforcements from neighboring towns.

It did not take long for the ranks of militiamen to swell to approximately 500. The militia began marching over the North Bridge toward town, where they encountered several British regiments. Shots rang out, and men fell on both sides. Gage's men were more interested in searching for weapons than fighting the militias. The British pulled back, and the militiamen hurried into defensive positions.

The British found few weapons in Concord and began returning to Boston, but the fighting was not over. More militiamen had arrived throughout the day. Between 3,000 and 4,000 militiamen hid in the woods along the road.[4] They shot at the returning British troops from the cover of brush and the tops of trees. The redcoats were not prepared for such an attack. If British reinforcements had not arrived from Boston, all the British troops that had gone to Concord that day would have been killed or taken prisoner. The American Revolution had begun.

**Colonists fought the British troops at the North Bridge outside of Concord.**

4

# DECLARING INDEPENDENCE

As night fell after the Battles of Lexington and Concord, many of the militiamen who followed the British back to Boston set up camp in the hills surrounding the bustling colonial city. They waited to see who would make the next move. For weeks, the colonies drifted between war and peace. The militiamen outside of Boston remained on alert.

In May 1775, the Second Continental Congress met in Philadelphia. The Congress was divided. Some delegates wanted to fight for independence while others still hoped to reconcile with Great Britain.

John Adams, one of Massachusetts's delegates, had no patience for reconciliation. "Powder and artillery are the most efficacious, sure, and infallible conciliatory measures we

General George Washington had proven his military skills during the French and Indian War. He was chosen to lead the Continental army.

> "Until an independence is declared, the continent will feel itself like a man who continues putting off some unpleasant business from day to day, yet knows it must be done, hates to set about it, wishes it over, and is continually haunted with the thoughts of its necessity."[3]
>
> —*Thomas Paine,* Common Sense

can adopt," he told the gathering.[1] The Congress agreed the colonies needed an army. At Adams's request, the Congress passed a resolution on June 14, recognizing the militias around Boston as the Continental army. This was America's first organized fighting force. On June 15, once again at Adams's urging, the Congress named 43-year-old George Washington the army's commander in chief.

The Second Continental Congress convened well into June 1775. In the meantime, the British army in Boston was getting restless. It was time for the British to make a move. They planned to attack the militiamen outside of Boston and force them from the hills surrounding the city.

## THE BATTLE OF BUNKER HILL

On June 17, 1775, Gage sent 2,400 troops up Breed's Hill, just north of Boston near Bunker Hill.[2] The Americans were ready for the attack. The patriots had managed to build fortifications very quickly. It was a hot and muggy day, and the redcoats struggled in the heat as they made their way up the hill. The militiamen waited behind dirt and brush fortifications. Just as the British reached the crest of the hill, the militia opened fire. Redcoats fell in great numbers. British troops soon retreated.

Then the British troops regrouped and charged the hill again. The militiamen held their ground, killing many more redcoats. Exhausted yet determined, the redcoats attempted a third attack on the militia's position. By this time, the patriots were running low on ammunition. A group of militiamen held off the British, giving the rest of the Americans time to retreat.

### MOVING TO BREED'S HILL

Patriot forces began building fortifications on Bunker Hill to prevent the British from extending their control outside the limits of Boston. The British learned about the construction and planned to attack the Americans before they dug in too deeply. Militia leaders realized their small cannons were not powerful enough to reach the enemy in Boston from Bunker Hill. So they ordered their men to move to Breed's Hill, roughly 2,000 feet (610 m) closer to the city. Most of the fighting took place on Breed's Hill, but when the Americans were finally forced to retreat, the British chased them to Bunker Hill. The British seized the hill, and the battle was named after the place where it ended.

The patriot forces held their fire until British forces were nearly upon them in the Battle of Bunker Hill.

The Battle of Bunker Hill, as the battle became known, was one of the bloodiest battles of the Revolutionary War. The Americans suffered 400 casualties, and more than 1,000 British soldiers were killed or wounded.[4]

The majority in the Second Continental Congress still hoped to avoid a full-blown war with Great Britain. On July 8, 1775, the Congress sent the Olive Branch Petition to King George. The petition encouraged the king to end hostilities and return to a state of harmony between Great Britain and the American colonies. The king rejected the plea. He went a step further by declaring the colonies to be in total rebellion against the crown.

### A FIERCE PATRIOT

After the Battle of Concord, Joseph Warren joined the militia members who were attacking the British as they tried to return to Boston. At the Battle of Bunker Hill, he took up arms and fought. When the British assaulted Breed's Hill for the third time, Warren stood front and center, engaging the redcoats in hand-to-hand combat. His bravery gave the retreating patriots time to escape. He was killed by British troops when they broke through the American line, but not before most of the Massachusetts militia had escaped to fight another day.

## A DIFFICULT CHOICE

Many colonists were opposed to the British Parliament's taxes and British military action. However, some of these same colonists remained loyal to the king. They were not ready to break away from their motherland. Choosing sides in the conflict was difficult for many colonial Americans. Many colonists considered themselves patriots and were committed to independence. Some remained loyal to Great Britain and were labeled loyalists. Other colonists remained neutral in the conflict. These conflicting loyalties divided communities, and it was difficult to know whom to trust.

The patriots' ranks were filled with merchants, artisans, landowners, farmers, and elected colonial officials. Patriots favored liberty, individual rights, and a voice in government.

Loyalists generally had stronger ties to Great Britain. Many loyalists had arrived in America just as tensions had begun building between their home country and the colonies. The newcomers were more accepting of the ways of the motherland than longtime colonists. Loyalists feared independence would lead to mob rule and violence.

Like other colonists, African Americans were divided in their loyalties. African Americans in the northern colonies, many of whom were already free, were more likely to join the patriots. However, in November 1775, British leaders offered freedom to any slaves who escaped from their American slave owners and joined the British army. Thousands of male slaves took the British at their word, fleeing from southern plantations to join British ranks. Soon after, the American army matched Great Britain's offer, and the Continental army's ranks began filling with African Americans.

For the most part, American Indians sided with the British. American Indians believed colonial settlers threatened their land much more than the British. However, some American Indian groups, such as the Oneidas in New York, helped the patriots. These American Indians served as scouts and soldiers. Other American Indian groups remained neutral, staying out of the war.

### AFRICAN AMERICANS IN THE FIGHT

By the time the Revolutionary War began, slavery had been going on in America for more than 100 years, but it was most common in the South. In Lexington and Concord, black men fought alongside white men to protect Massachusetts. But in mid-1775, under pressure from some southern political leaders, General Washington issued an order banning African Americans from serving in the Continental army. Later that year, both the Congress and Washington realized that the army's manpower shortage was so severe that African Americans were needed to join the patriot cause. Washington lifted the ban.

## MOVING TOWARD INDEPENDENCE

King George may have rejected the peace attempt, but the colonies did not declare independence immediately. Ever since it had convened in May 1775, the Second Continental Congress had been acting as the government of the colonies. One of its major tasks was finding a way to raise the money needed to fight a war against mighty Great Britain. The Congress had no power to tax the colonies to pay for the army and related expenses. Instead, the Congress had to request funds from the colonies. The colonies, which had expenses of their own, were not always willing to donate money.

The Congress had also not officially declared independence from Great Britain. That was a difficult task because delegates needed the authority from their individual colonial governments to vote in favor of breaking from British rule. Getting such authority was taking months.

Meanwhile, the British had maintained control of Boston since the Battle of Bunker Hill. General Washington devised a plan to force the British from the city. In November 1775, Washington ordered artillery from Fort Ticonderoga be brought to Dorchester Heights, an area overlooking Boston and Boston Harbor. He hoped to force the British into a fight. In March 1776, the artillery was finally put in place. The British realized it threatened their naval supply lines. Recognizing they could not hold onto Boston much longer, the British left the city.

Washington's move had bolstered the revolutionary spirit. The British departure from Boston was seen as a major victory for the patriots. A five-member committee, led by Thomas

On August 2, 1776, the members of Congress began signing the Declaration of Independence.

Jefferson, began writing the Declaration of Independence in June 1776. The Congress passed a resolution of independence on July 2. Then, after much debate, the Congress adopted the Declaration of Independence on July 4, establishing the United States of America. A new free nation, made up of 13 states, was born. But the British were not leaving without a fight.

5

# EARLY STRUGGLES

When the British left Boston in March 1776, General Washington knew the redcoats' next objective would be to capture New York City. In April, he had ordered American troops to move from Boston to New York. Washington was not sure he had the manpower to defend New York, but the Congress felt he had to try. British military commanders did not waste any time, either. They started sending troops to New York in early spring 1776, setting out on a collision course with the Continental army.

General William Howe was now in charge of the British army in America. His brother, Admiral Richard Howe, was commanding the Royal Navy in North America. On June 29, 1776, less than a week before the Second Continental Congress adopted the Declaration of Independence, Admiral Howe arrived in Staten Island, New York. The admiral brought 10,000 men, 30 warships, and 100 transport ships with him.[1] From his

A mob of patriots in New York tore down a statue of King George after a public reading of the Declaration of Independence.

Great Britain was ready for a fight in the summer of 1776, with the British navy assembled in full force off Staten Island.

window in Manhattan, one man was stunned to see the British ships sailing toward New York: "I could not believe my eyes . . . the whole bay was as full of shipping as it ever could be, I declare that I thought all of London was afloat."[2]

Admiral Howe's fleet was just part of the 32,000 British troops that would eventually assemble in Staten Island.[3] By mid-August, more warships had joined the fleet. It was the largest force Great Britain had ever sent into a military action.

## PREPARING FOR WAR

General Howe was not committed to an immediate attack. He was under orders to try to negotiate a peace settlement with the Americans, and he attempted to do just that in late July. Howe had the power to grant pardons to rebels who surrendered. He even made an offer to pardon Washington if he gave up the fight. The American commander in chief, however, stated, "Those who have committed no fault want no pardon."[4]

When peace failed, Howe prepared for war. So did Washington and his army of 19,000 men, most of whom were far from battle-ready.[5] The American forces were divided between Long Island and Manhattan. On August 22, Howe sent 20,000 men from Staten Island to the southern shore of Long Island.[6] From there, the British would march north and west to attack the Continental army, which occupied Brooklyn Heights. This would be the Americans' first major battle under Washington's command.

## THE BATTLE OF LONG ISLAND

American intelligence reported three ways into Brooklyn Heights. General Washington ordered American forces to guard all three routes. He knew nothing about Jamaica Pass, a fourth way into Brooklyn Heights. As a result, American soldiers were not guarding the pass.

Loyalist spies told General Howe about the unguarded Jamaica Pass. Howe quickly devised a plan. The British would attack the Americans with smaller forces at the guarded pathways. The bulk of the redcoats would head to Jamaica Pass and launch a surprise attack.

After night fell on August 26, approximately 10,000 British troops moved to Jamaica Pass.[7] Cannon fire broke the silence of the dawn on August 27. The British attack was underway. The Jamaica Pass assault caught the Continental army completely off guard. The patriots were soon surrounded. American losses quickly mounted. By 11:00 a.m., the battle was nearly over.

Washington's troops decided to retreat. But they could not escape without some type of cover from the unrelenting British attack. A regiment of soldiers from Maryland, known as the Maryland 400, stood their ground and provided the needed cover. As gunfire whistled around them for three grueling hours, the Maryland 400 held off thousands of Great Britain's best soldiers. The Maryland soldiers' bravery allowed the remaining American troops to escape. None of the 400 turned and ran. Even the British marveled at the soldiers' courage on the battlefield.

### ARMED AND DANGEROUS

Soldiers on both sides of the Revolutionary War relied mostly on muskets on the battlefield. Muskets fired heavy lead balls, which were good at repelling enemies at close range. Loading a musket took four steps, but experienced soldiers could do it in less than 15 seconds. Muskets were sometimes equipped with a 21-inch (53 cm), three-sided bayonet. Bayonets were capable of inflicting severe wounds.

Eventually, however, the British overcame the Maryland 400. Most of the regiment was killed, wounded, or captured. However, the bravery of the soldiers ensured the survival of the newly formed Continental army. The surviving American troops escaped to the East River. The British had won what became known as the Battle of Long Island.

General Howe did not order his men to pursue the Americans. He felt the Royal Navy could capture the remaining American troops at the river's mouth. However, over the next

## RISKY MISSION

After the British surprise attack at the Battle of Long Island, General Washington realized he needed to know more about the British troops. In September 1776, he asked for a volunteer to go behind enemy lines to spy on the British. Nathan Hale, a 21-year-old first lieutenant from Connecticut, was the only volunteer. Disguised as a schoolteacher, Hale began his mission on September 8. He crossed the river into Manhattan, which by then was under British control. Once there, Hale drew maps of British troop locations. The British discovered he was a spy on September 21, and Hale was arrested and hanged the next day. Hale's final words inspired the entire nation: "I only regret that I have but one life to lose for my country."[8]

two days, a heavy storm with strong winds prevented the Royal Navy from reaching the Americans. The British army kept a watchful eye on the patriots, but they were not worried. With the river behind them, they believed the Americans could not escape.

## A STEALTHY ESCAPE

When the storm ended, a thick, soupy fog covered the Long Island shore. The fog made it hard for the redcoats to see the American soldiers on the Long Island shoreline. General Washington used the fog to his advantage. He ordered his supply officer to find every transport boat on both sides of the East River. Most of the watercraft were rowboats. After night fell on August 29, Washington began evacuating

# STORIES FROM THE WAR

Joseph Plumb Martin was an American soldier from Milford, Connecticut, who participated in General Washington's bold escape from Long Island to Manhattan on August 29, 1776. He wrote about the escape in his diary:

**"In the latter part of the afternoon, there fell a very heavy shower of rain, which wet us all to the skin and much damaged our ammunition. . . . At about ten P.M., when darkness had set in, the regiments began marching down to the ferry. We are strictly enjoined not to speak, not even cough, while on the march. All orders were given from officer to officer, and communicated to the men in whispers. What such secrecy could mean we could not divine. We marched off in the same way that we had come onto the island, forming various conjectures among ourselves as to our destination."[9]**

his troops from Long Island to Manhattan, aided by darkness and fog. After six hours of rowing back and forth between Manhattan and Long Island, all of Washington's men were evacuated. As dawn broke on August 30, the skies cleared. The British woke to find the Americans had escaped.

Washington's army lost the rest of New York by mid-September. They continued losing the battles that followed. The American troops retreated through parts of upstate New York and New Jersey. By December 1776, the Continental army had fallen back to Pennsylvania. Battered but not broken, Washington's men had a tough winter ahead.

The Continental army's daring nighttime escape was a victory for the patriots, even though they had lost the battle for Long Island.

6

# A STIRRING COMEBACK

As 1776 came to a close, General Washington feared his army would not be able to keep up the fight. The Continental army was shrinking. The troop strength under Washington's command, once 19,000 men strong, was down to 5,000.[1] Many had been killed, wounded, or captured in the many battles lost to the British. Others had deserted the army, convinced they were fighting for a lost cause.

The tours of duty for several thousand troops ended in late November, and they refused to reenlist. More enlistments would end by the close of December. Many of the remaining American troops were ill with dysentery from drinking dirty water. Smallpox was sweeping through the patriots' military camps. Washington knew what the Americans needed most

Washington's victory at the Battle of Princeton in January 1777 helped boost patriot morale.

was a decisive victory in battle. With winter upon them, Washington's soldiers were now in Pennsylvania. Food and medical supplies were low.

The British were spending the winter in New York. They also had outposts south and west of the city. One outpost was in stone barracks in Trenton, New Jersey, near the Delaware River. This was just ten miles (16 km) from where Washington and his troops were camped in Pennsylvania. Approximately 1,500 skilled Hessian soldiers guarded the British outpost.[2]

## A CHRISTMAS SURPRISE

General Washington felt it was only a matter of time before the British attacked his troops in Pennsylvania, so he chose to make the first move. On December 25, 1776, the general decided to cross the partially frozen Delaware River and capture Trenton. Packed in flimsy boats, the Continental army began the risky crossing in frigid temperatures. The men had to steer around large floating blocks of ice, capable of smashing the American boats, before they got close to shore.

By the time Washington's men reached the shores of New Jersey in the early morning hours of December 26, snow was falling. Still, Washington and his troops soldiered on.

The harsh conditions of the Delaware River slowed Washington's crossing.

The Americans marched nine miles (14 km) to the British outpost in Trenton. Two of Washington's men froze to death on the way.

The Continental army reached the outpost just as dawn broke. They found the Hessians still asleep in their barracks. The Americans surrounded the barracks, and the soldiers' opening shots shattered the morning silence. Some of the Hessian troops ran away. Most put up a fight, but the Continental army outnumbered them. Within an hour, Washington had his victory.

The Americans captured approximately 900 enemy troops and killed or wounded approximately 100.[3] The triumph at Trenton energized the American troops, and many men agreed

Hessian colonel Johann Rall quickly realized his men were outnumbered and surrendered to Washington.

to reenlist. Americans were heartened by another victory at the Battle of Princeton just one week later. But many more troops would still be needed.

## TROOP SHORTAGES

By the end of 1776, troop shortages became critical for the Americans. Washington felt it was essential the British never find out about the dwindling Continental army. He circulated false reports about the number of men he had under his command. The British believed the inflated numbers, especially after the swift American victory in Trenton.

The Congress offered land, money, and even a new suit of clothes to men who enlisted in the military, but few showed any interest. Finally, in 1777, the Congress began giving states quotas for the number of men they would have to provide to the Continental army. This led many states to enact a draft. Those drafted would have to serve in the army or send someone to take their places. Those who refused to do either would have to pay a heavy fine.

## AMERICA'S ARMY

Single boys and men with little property or responsibilities often sold their services to men who did not want to serve in the army. Most of America's soldiers were poor men who did not have enough money to buy their way out of military service. The officers were the only men of wealth in the Continental army.

As they waited for more recruits after the Battles of Trenton and Princeton, Washington's men spent the early part of 1777 in Morristown, New Jersey. Covered by heavy brush and surrounded by hills in the northwest corner of the state, Morristown was the perfect location for Washington's troops to regroup and heal. But the Continental army was keenly aware that the enemy, hunkered down in New York City, was just a day's march away.

# ON THE FRONT LINES

## BATTLE OF PRINCETON

The British could not ignore the Continental army's victory in Trenton. General Howe sent General Charles Cornwallis and 8,000 men to defeat what was left of the Continental army.[4]

Cornwallis arrived in Princeton, New Jersey, from New York City in the waning days of 1776. General Washington had taken up a position just south of Trenton, near Assunpink Creek. In the early morning hours of January 2, 1777, Cornwallis divided his force. He led the majority of his men to Trenton to engage Washington. After marching 12 hours in heavy mud, Cornwallis's men came near Washington's camp. However, the British troops were exhausted from the long march, and the general decided to wait until morning to attack the Americans.

Washington took advantage of the delay. That night, the general quietly gathered his men. He sent most of them to Princeton to attack the British troops. Others stayed behind to keep campfires burning so the British would not realize anyone was gone.

On the way to Princeton in the dawn of January 3, Washington's men encountered a group of British soldiers on

Washington led the Continental army to victory at the Battle of Princeton.

their way to reinforce Cornwallis. Washington led the daring attack himself. As bullets flew around him, he rallied his men to defeat the enemy, and they did. Washington's forces continued on to Princeton, where they beat back the British once again. Cornwallis withdrew to New Brunswick, New Jersey, the last British outpost in that state.

7

# THE WAR RAGES ON

American forces were beginning to string together victories on the battlefield. In the meantime, the Second Continental Congress was trying to win support from countries around the world for the struggling nation's revolutionary cause. France was an obvious first choice as a possible ally.

France had considered entering the fray from the very beginning. The country was anxious for the chance to take on and defeat its longtime rival, Great Britain. France had been secretly giving the United States aid, mainly in the form of weapons and loans, since the conflict began. But to win the Revolutionary War, the patriots needed more aid. The new

The American alliance with France, settled with the Treaty of Alliance in Paris in February 1778, would help change the course of the war for the struggling patriots.

nation hoped the French would commit to the war, sending ground troops and naval support to aid the Americans.

## PUSHING FOR FOREIGN SUPPORT

In March 1777, an American delegation, led by 71-year-old Benjamin Franklin, went to Paris. Franklin's goal was to secure a commitment from France to join with the patriots in the Revolutionary War. Franklin worked hard to persuade the French the newly formed nation could win the war. He hoped if France became America's ally, it would turn the tide of the war in the patriots' favor. The British hoped they could end the war before France committed.

### MONSIEUR FRANKLIN

Benjamin Franklin was a man of many talents. He is remembered as a politician, inventor, diplomat, author, scientist, and founding father of the United States. As a member of the Second Continental Congress, he served on the committee that helped write the Declaration of Independence. Well known in France for his inventions and writings, Franklin was the perfect choice to send to Paris. The charming and witty Franklin fascinated the French people, who invited him to parties and political events. There, he worked hard to gain support for the patriot cause.

One Frenchman who needed no convincing was

the wealthy, 19-year-old Marquis de Lafayette. A member of a military family, the young Lafayette understood warfare. In April 1777, Lafayette purchased a ship and set sail for America. He arrived in mid-June and headed to Philadelphia. When Lafayette said he would serve in the Continental army without pay, the Congress made him a major general and sent him to meet with General Washington, who was stationed nearby. Washington quickly recognized Lafayette's keen military instinct.

Meanwhile, the British began implementing their plan to cut off New England from the rest of the 13 colonies, a military action that would lead to the Battle of Saratoga. General Howe left New York City in June to get in position to participate in that battle. However, he decided to change direction and capture Philadelphia, which was serving as the new nation's capital, before heading to upstate New York.

## THE BATTLES OF BRANDYWINE AND GERMANTOWN

General Washington believed he could stop the British advance before the redcoats reached Philadelphia. He lined up his men along the Brandywine Creek just outside the city.

The Americans planned to fend off the British along the creek banks and keep them out of the capital. Washington covered what he thought were all the creek crossings. But Howe found a shallow crossing approximately 12 miles (19 km) north of where Washington's men were stationed.

In the early morning of September 11, 1777, Howe's troops encountered the Continental army. The Americans thought they were under attack by the entire British force, but Howe had actually sent a large portion of his army north to the crossing he found. A heavy fog covered the area, allowing the redcoats to cross unnoticed. Once they reached the other side of the creek, the British surrounded the Americans. The battle that followed was hard fought and bloody. Washington's men suffered heavy losses, and only nightfall brought the battle to an end.

Lafayette was shot in the leg but stayed in the battle. He guided an organized retreat that saved many American lives. The patriots had lost the Battle of Brandywine. The British troops did not pursue the retreating Americans because "night and the fatigue the soldiers had undergone prevented any pursuit," according to British Captain John Andre.[1] The redcoats regrouped in time to march into Philadelphia on

Americans fought fiercely at the Battle of Brandywine, but they ultimately lost the battle to the British.

September 26 and capture the city. The Americans could not mount a defense.

However, the intensity with which the Americans fought at the Battle of Brandywine prompted General Howe to stay in Philadelphia. He expected a patriot offensive attack. As a result, he never got to the Battle of Saratoga, contributing to the major British defeat.

Howe was right about an impending American attack. Many British troops were stationed in Germantown, Pennsylvania, just outside Philadelphia. On October 4, 1777, Washington launched a surprise attack on the town. The Continental army was winning the battle most of the day, but the Americans had to retreat when fog rolled in and ammunition ran low. However, that setback was overshadowed by the stunning American victory at Saratoga.

Word soon reached France about the devastating British defeat at the Battle of Saratoga. The battle would largely be viewed as the turning point in the Revolutionary War, in part because it brought France into the war as an American ally. After the victory, the French king Louis XVI began negotiating an alliance with the Americans. A treaty was signed, and France recognized the new nation on February 6, 1778.

## A BRUTAL WINTER

French assistance would arrive in spring 1778. However, before help came, the Continental army spent an agonizing winter in southeast Pennsylvania. Following the Battles of Brandywine and Germantown, General Washington selected a wooded area in Valley Forge, Pennsylvania, 20 miles (32 km) west of

Philadelphia, to set up a winter camp. From there, his forces could watch British troop movements in Philadelphia.

The hardships the Continental army bore during the harsh winter of 1777 to 1778 would be greater than anything it endured in battle. Ice and frigid winds battered the troops on a daily basis. Blankets were in short supply, and soldiers' clothing was thin and tattered. There was usually little food, and sometimes there was no food at all. The struggling nation simply had no money to spend on its army.

### FRIENDS AND ALLIES

The Oneidas, American Indians living in upstate New York, helped the United States win the Battle of Saratoga by fighting alongside the Continental army. When Oneida Chief Oskanondonha heard of the food shortage at Valley Forge, he sent some of his warriors with 600 bushels of dry corn to feed the soldiers. The Oneidas walked hundreds of miles to reach Valley Forge. One Oneida woman, known as Polly Cooper, came along to cook the corn. Forty-seven Oneida warriors stayed at Valley Forge to join the battle against the British. The Oneidas were America's first allies.

Of the 11,000 men who went with Washington to Valley Forge, approximately 2,000 died of starvation, disease or froze to death.[2] Another 2,000 men deserted.[3] However, amid

Washington, Lafayette, and the rest of the Continental army faced a cold and brutal winter in Valley Forge.

the suffering, there was one bright spot for the Continental army. In February 1778, Baron Friedrich Wilhelm von Steuben arrived at Valley Forge, bringing much-needed expertise in handling weapons and training soldiers. An experienced

Prussian military man, Steuben volunteered to train the undisciplined Continental army. He taught the men military tactics, the importance of following orders, and how to effectively use a bayonet. Steuben even established a sanitary code for the camp. He gave the American troops fresh confidence. By the spring, having survived an even greater foe than the British, Washington's men were ready for the battles ahead.

## WOMEN AT WAR

Some women followed their husbands, sons, brothers, and fathers into combat. These women felt they belonged beside their loved ones wherever they were, including on the battlefield. Women usually stayed far behind the battle lines. They helped out by cooking meals and washing and mending clothes. Women at Valley Forge stayed in cabins built especially for them, but they had no blankets and little food. General Washington's wife, Martha, made the trip to Valley Forge from the family's home in Mount Vernon, Virginia. She brought a wagon loaded with food and supplies, including cloth, wool, sewing materials, and medicine. After arriving on February 3, 1778, she organized the women in the camp to tend to the needs of the soldiers, including making socks and shirts.

8

# CHANGING STRATEGY

By the spring of 1778, Great Britain had a new battle plan. Because the British had not ended the war quickly, the Americans had time to recruit France as an ally. General Howe had fought the war cautiously, and British leaders were tired of his approach. Now King George wanted to aggressively end the Revolutionary War.

In May 1778, General Henry Clinton replaced Howe as commander in chief. His second-in-command was General Charles Cornwallis. Fearing the Continental army would now attack New York City with the aid of France, the British Parliament ordered Clinton to leave Philadelphia and bring all British troops and equipment to Manhattan. Most of the equipment went by ship, but British troops would march from

The patriots launched an offensive against the British at the Battle of Monmouth in June 1778, hoping to attack British troops before they had a chance to attack the Americans.

Philadelphia to Manhattan through New Jersey. In a column eight miles (13 km) long, more than 10,000 redcoats marched across New Jersey.[1] General Washington watched from afar. On June 28, as the British neared Monmouth in central New Jersey, Washington decided to launch an offensive.

## THE BATTLE OF MONMOUTH

General Washington's army had approximately 13,000 men, and they were supported by 6,000 local New Jersey militia troops.[2] Washington's plan hit a bump when one of his columns of troops failed to attack as ordered and retreated instead. Washington quickly stepped in and rallied the troops to make a strong stand on the Monmouth battlefield. When the smoke cleared on that hot summer night, neither side could claim victory. On the British side, approximately 300 men were killed or wounded, and many more were captured or deserted. The Americans suffered 350 dead, wounded, or missing.[3] This would prove to be the last major battle up north.

The British moved toward New York City overnight. After the lengthy battle in Monmouth, Washington decided not to pursue. Two weeks later, the patriots learned a French fleet had arrived in Philadelphia via the Delaware River.

The Americans devised a plan to strike the British naval base in Newport, Rhode Island, by land and sea, with the help of the French navy. It would be the first joint effort in the war by the Americans and the French.

The mission was set for August 8, but stormy weather prevented French warships from getting into position in time. The attack was called off. Before another plan was developed, the Continental army learned the British were turning their attention southward.

## THE SOUTHERN STRATEGY

With the war having reached a stalemate in the North, the British decided to take the fight to Georgia, Virginia, North Carolina, and South Carolina. The plan was to capture the South and sweep through the North to claim victory. Lieutenant Colonel Archibald Campbell would

### DIVIDED LOYALTIES

South Carolina had nearly as many loyalists as patriots. There were few places in America where the two sides were so evenly divided and willing to do battle. The fighting between loyalists and patriots was bitter and bloody. There were skirmishes every day between the two sides, especially in the backcountry. Neighbor fought against neighbor. The conflict plunged South Carolina into a state of civil war.

lead the British troops in the South. Southern loyalists who knew the terrain well would assist the British.

The redcoats put their plan into action in late 1778. More than 3,600 British troops attacked Savannah, Georgia, on December 29.[4] With less than 900 American militiamen on hand to defend the city, it did not take long for the British to secure a victory.[5] This was a crushing defeat for the Americans. With French assistance, Americans tried recapturing the city in the fall of 1779. But by that time, the British had built up their defenses. The second Battle of Savannah, on October 9, 1779, ended in disaster for the patriots. Great Britain now had a firm hold on Georgia.

Secure with the battles they had already won in the

### BIG GUNS

The cannon was considered cutting-edge artillery technology during the American Revolution. Land troops that did not have at least one cannon usually lost battles. Cannons came in various sizes. Lightweight cannons were mounted on wooden wheels and moved across battlefields. Heavier cannons were mounted and used inside forts. Cannons shot three types of projectiles. Solid cannonballs were mostly used to destroy fortifications. Exploding projectiles were filled with explosives. Scattered shot discharged small, sharp objects in all different directions. Exploding projectiles and scattered shot were used to attack troops.

Cannons, such as these at Valley Forge, were important weapons for both sides during the Revolutionary War.

South, the British army was ready to go after another port city, Charleston, South Carolina. The British began a well-planned siege of Charleston in early April 1780, landing troops from the sea. The redcoats relentlessly attacked the outnumbered Continental army and local militias. The British pounded the city with fierce artillery fire, damaging military fortifications and many homes. After nearly six weeks of fighting, the Americans surrendered on May 12.

The defeat shook the revolutionary cause. More than 3,000 Americans were taken prisoner, practically wiping out the

Continental army in the South.[6] The British were convinced the Americans had no strength in the South and had been defeated.

The Continental army rushed more troops from New York to South Carolina in an attempt to stop the British in Camden, South Carolina, 115 miles (185 km) northwest of Charleston. The British were setting up a supply storehouse there. The battle that broke out on August 16, 1780, ended in another defeat for the Continental army. Another 1,000 Americans were captured, approximately 900 were killed, and a large amount of supplies were lost.[7]

The redcoats were ready to focus their attention on returning to the North, but the Americans were not ready to give up the South. Local militias continued assaulting the British. Led by seasoned fighters, the militiamen launched small, well-planned attacks. The southern militias struck the British when they least expected it. These raids caused heavy enemy casualties and prevented the British from gaining full control of South Carolina.

## THE BATTLE OF KING'S MOUNTAIN

A group of these homegrown fighters delivered a major patriot victory at the Battle of King's Mountain in York County, South

## STORIES FROM THE WAR

Garret Watts served in the North Carolina militia and fought in the Battle of Camden. Years later, he recalled his experiences in the battle:

**"I remember that I was among the nearest to the enemy . . . that we had orders to wait for the word to commence firing; that the militia were in front and in a feeble condition at that time. They were fatigued. The weather was warm excessively. They had been fed a short time previously on molasses entirely. I can state on oath that I believe my gun was the first gun fired, notwithstanding the orders, for we were close to the enemy, who appeared to maneuver in contempt of us, and I fired without thinking except that I might prevent the man opposite from killing me. The discharge and loud roar soon became general from one end of the lines to the other. Amongst other things, I confess I was amongst the first that fled. The cause of this I cannot tell, except that everyone I saw was about to do the same. . . . There was no effort to rally, no encouragement to fight. Officers and men joined in the flight."[8]**

Carolina. In October 1780, General Cornwallis sent a group of fighters with British Major Patrick Ferguson to the South Carolina–North Carolina border. He hoped to track down some of the patriot militia fighters. Ferguson's men set up camp on King's Mountain.

Members of the North Carolina militia were not about to let the British catch up with them. On October 7, they surrounded King's Mountain and attacked. Southern American militias were made up of frontiersmen who were excellent shots. They killed Ferguson and killed or captured the rest of his force. The loss was a major setback for the British. It proved the Americans had not yet lost the South.

Also in October, General Washington sent General Nathanael Greene to command troops in the South. Greene took General Daniel Morgan with him. Morgan was a well-respected soldier who had contributed mightily to the American victory at the Battle of Saratoga.

Morgan engineered major offensive attacks in the South. He first masterminded a strategic victory at the Battle of Cowpens in South Carolina on January 17, 1781. Then Greene and Morgan combined forces to deliver a devastating blow to the British at Guilford Courthouse in North Carolina on March 15. The British

The southern militias' victory over the British at the Battle of King's Mountain was an important win for the patriots.

suffered more than 500 casualties in the battle.[9] Cornwallis then made the fateful decision to lead his men to Yorktown, Virginia, to fight the battle of their lives.

# ON THE FRONT LINES
## BATTLE OF COWPENS

In January 1781, General Morgan took some troops and went to the South Carolina countryside. His mission was to get supplies and recruit militia fighters to support the efforts of the Continental army. Morgan's reputation alone was enough to persuade many militiamen to join him.

Morgan had been working just south of the North Carolina border, and loyalists reported Morgan's activity to General Cornwallis. In response, Cornwallis sent troops under the command of young Lieutenant Colonel Banastre Tarleton to stop him. While on a routine patrol near the North Carolina border, members of the Continental army captured some loyalists, who told them about Cornwallis's plan.

Morgan decided to take on the British. He let the redcoats get close to him, but he kept moving until he reached a location he felt favored his troops. The position was a local cattle-grazing field called Cowpens. Morgan set up camp there and waited for the British to attack. He put his sharpshooters, excellent marksmen, on the front line. Morgan ordered them to unleash two volleys of shots at the approaching redcoats and then step aside to let the Continental army attack the broken British ranks. The militiamen would then circle around and back up the army.

Morgan's plan worked. Tarleton could not wait to attack. He ordered his troops, already tired from chasing Morgan for days, to charge. They immediately faltered under the heavy militia fire and then collapsed when the rest of the American forces charged them. Cowpens turned the southern Revolutionary War in the patriots' favor and reinvigorated the Continental army.

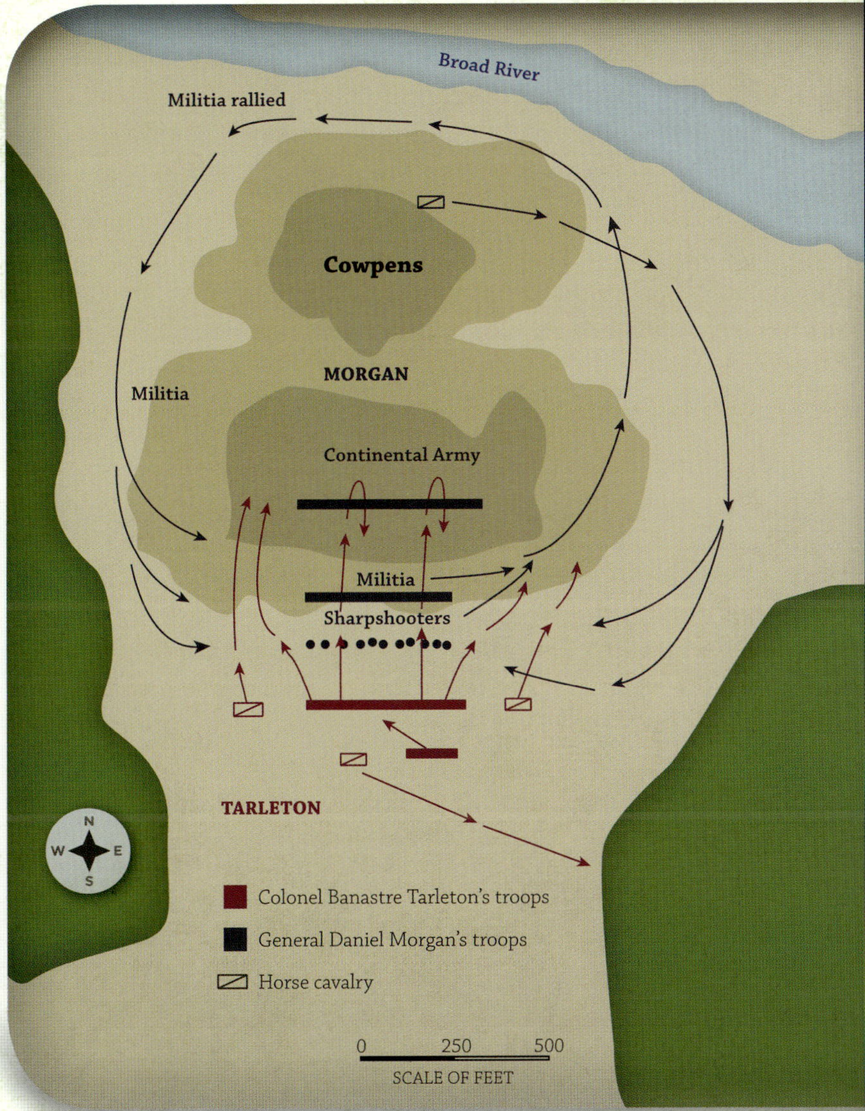

9

# VICTORY AND PEACE

Fed up with fighting in the Carolinas, General Cornwallis set his sights on invading Virginia. He arrived with his troops at the river port of Yorktown, Virginia, near the Chesapeake Bay, in early August 1781 and set up camp. Cornwallis felt this could be a decisive battle in the war and asked General Clinton in New York City for more troops. Clinton refused, convinced Cornwallis's 7,200 men could hold off any challenge and believing the Americans were preparing to attack New York City.[1]

The American troops had been outnumbered in Yorktown, but General Washington sent the French general Lafayette to the port with substantial reinforcements. He also sent French troops from Rhode Island who had been waiting to do battle.

By late summer 1781, the Revolutionary War was nearly over, and the patriots effectively ended the war with the Battle of Yorktown in October.

By the time all the troops arrived in Virginia in late September, the patriot ground force amounted to approximately 17,000 men.[2] The French navy made its way to Chesapeake Bay to form a blockade.

Cornwallis was in a poor defensive position at the center of the port. As Washington's men made their way to Yorktown, they blocked all British escape routes. Once the French navy arrived in the Chesapeake Bay, it cut off Cornwallis from any British naval support.

### THE AMERICANS ARE COMING

In an attempt to keep the British off guard, General Washington let it be known he intended to attack New York City in late 1781. The misinformation was a major reason General Clinton refused to send reinforcements from New York to Yorktown. Meanwhile, Washington was secretly moving the bulk of his troops to Yorktown.

## THE FINAL STAND

At the end of September, the British could see the large American-French force marching toward Yorktown. There was nowhere for the redcoats to go. All they could do was fortify their position. On October 9, Washington ordered his troops to start firing the army's several hundred cannons at the

Cornwallis officially surrendered to Washington at 2:00 p.m. on October 19.

British. Cornwallis was shocked at the American troops' firepower, especially since the Continental army had used only a small number of cannons in the past. With the support of the French, America had much more artillery.

In a letter to Clinton, Cornwallis wrote about the attack: "The fire continued . . . until all our guns on the left were silenced . . . and our loss of men considerable."[3] On October 14, American and French troops attacked and overtook some major British defensive positions. The bombardment continued until the early morning hours of October 17, when the British waved a white flag of surrender.

This was more than the end of a battle. It would be the end of a war. Minor battles continued for a while, but the British were frustrated after the Battle of Yorktown. The British Parliament had lost interest in America. It felt the war was too costly. British citizens also thought it made no economic sense to maintain an army 3,000 miles (4,800 km) away. The lower house of the Parliament passed a resolution in February 1782, ending all British land attacks in America.

## PEACE TALKS

With the end of the physical battles came the difficult task of negotiating peace between the two sides. Peace talks began in Paris on April 12, 1782. Founding fathers Benjamin Franklin, John Adams, and John Jay represented the United States in the lengthy negotiations. The initial sticking point was Britain's refusal to grant the country full independence. The three American negotiators would not discuss any aspect of a peace treaty until Great Britain agreed to this point. The British negotiators finally conceded approximately two months later.

Benjamin Franklin, *right*, played an important role in negotiating the Treaty of Paris with British representative Richard Oswald, *left*.

By the end of November 1782, a preliminary peace agreement was reached. The agreement was finalized on September 3, 1783, with the signing of the Treaty of Paris, which granted the United States full independence from Britain. In addition to establishing the conditions for peace, the Treaty of Paris outlined the geographic boundaries for the new nation. The United States ran east to west from the Atlantic Ocean to the Mississippi River and north to south from Canada to the northern border of Florida.

The treaty cleared the way for British troops to leave New York City. The final boatload of British troops left Manhattan Island on November 25, 1783. General Washington then marched victoriously into New York City with members of the Continental army.

The United States of America was now a free and internationally recognized nation, but independence had its own set of problems. The war had left the young country in great debt. The new nation had borrowed heavily from foreign countries to fund the war. It owed $160 million. If the country did not pay it back, the government would not be able to borrow any more money. The central government lacked the power to tax, and little money was being raised at the national level. As a result, many who served in the Continental army toward the end of the war were never paid. There would be little time for America to rejoice over winning its independence from Great Britain. The enormous task of building a nation beckoned.

## BUILDING A GOVERNMENT

The fledgling United States faced the enormous task of setting up a national government. The American people feared giving a national government too much power; therefore, the central government that guided the country through the Revolutionary War was relatively weak. It needed to be strengthened to govern a growing nation. If not, states might pursue their own interests and break apart into smaller republics.

### FREEDOM FOR SOME

Many American Indians were displaced during the Revolutionary War and never got their land back. After the war, settlers hurried to settle American Indian lands that were outside the boundaries of the new nation. Conflicts between the settlers and American Indians would continue for centuries. Many African-American slaves who fought in the war were reclaimed or recaptured by slave owners. Free African Americans continued battling prejudice and discrimination, despite the sacrifices they made during the war. There was no easy way to address these inequalities, and the United States would wrestle with these issues for decades to come.

After the Revolutionary War, the new country also faced the enormous task of establishing a strong national government to properly manage a growing, unified nation. In May 1787, a Constitutional Convention convened in Philadelphia. Every state but Rhode Island sent delegates. The convention's task

## THE ARTICLES OF CONFEDERATION

Before the United States Constitution went into effect on March 4, 1789, the Articles of Confederation governed the nation. Established in 1777 by the Second Continental Congress, the Articles of Confederation were not adopted by all 13 colonies-turned-states until 1781. The Congress used the document to run a national government during the Revolutionary War, even as the states were still in the process of ratifying it. The Articles of Confederation created a weak form of government. The young nation had no executive branch and no national court system. The document did not give the central government any way to enforce the laws it made or the power to tax. However, the Articles of Confederation did give the federal government the power to declare war, make peace, and sign treaties.

was to write a constitution that would govern the United States. After four months of debate, the new Constitution was unveiled.

The carefully crafted document protected states' rights while giving the national government the power it needed to run the country. The Constitution created a federal government with three branches—executive, legislative, and judicial. After the Constitution was ratified by the states, the new government became a reality in March 1789. A month later, the nation elected as its first president General George Washington. Washington was already a respected leader,

We the People of the United States, in Order to form a more perfect Union, establish Jus
ure domestic Tranquility, provide for the common defence, promote the general Welfare, and secure the Blessings of Liberty to ourselv
d our Posterity, do ordain and establish this Constitution for the United States of America.

Article. I.

ection. 1. All legislative Powers herein granted shall be vested in a Congress of the United States, which shall consist of a Senate and Ho
f Representatives.
ection. 2. The House of Representatives shall be composed of Members chosen every second Year by the People of the several States, and the E
each State shall have the Qualifications requisite for Electors of the most numerous Branch of the State Legislature.
No Person shall be a Representative who shall not have attained to the Age of twenty five Years, and been seven Years a Citizen of the United S
nd who shall not, when elected, be an Inhabitant of that State in which he shall be chosen.
Representatives and direct Taxes shall be apportioned among the several States which may be included within this Union, according to their respecti
umbers, which shall be determined by adding to the whole Number of free Persons, including those bound to Service for a Term of Years, and excluding In
t taxed, three fifths of all other Persons. The actual Enumeration shall be made within three Years after the first Meeting of the Congress of the Unite
d within every subsequent Term of ten Years, in such Manner as they shall by Law direct. The Number of Representatives shall not exceed one for
rty Thousand, but each State shall have at Least one Representative; and until such enumeration shall be made, the State of New Hampshire sha
titled to chuse three, Massachusetts eight, Rhode Island and Providence Plantations one, Connecticut five, New York six, New Jersey four, Pennsylv

The US Constitution became the foundation for the United States.

and government leaders hoped he could ease the transition into the government under the new Constitution.

The Constitution's most important attribute was its flexibility; the document could be amended. This flexibility allowed the US government to grow and change with the country for more than two centuries. At the same time, the Constitution would always protect the freedoms the patriots had fought so hard for in the Revolutionary War.

## 1770

The Boston Massacre takes place on March 5, sparking the American colonists' desire for independence from Great Britain.

## 1773

The Boston Tea Party takes place on December 16, contributing to the start of the Revolutionary War.

## 1774

The British Parliament orders Boston Harbor closed in March.

## 1775

Shots are fired in Lexington, Massachusetts, and then in Concord, starting the Revolutionary War on April 19.

## 1775

The Second Continental Congress names George Washington commander in chief of the Continental army on June 15.

## 1775

The Battle of Bunker Hill, just outside of Boston, takes place on June 17.

## 1776

The Second Continental Congress adopts the Declaration of Independence on July 4.

**1776**

The Battle of Long Island, which eventually leads to the British capture of New York City, begins on August 27.

**1776**

The patriots win the Battle of Trenton in New Jersey on December 26.

**1777**

British troops surrender at the Second Battle of Saratoga on October 17.

**1778**

France becomes a US ally in the Revolutionary War on February 6.

**1780**

The Continental army loses the Battle of Charleston, South Carolina, on May 12.

**1781**

A major turning point in the war takes place when the Continental army gets a strategic victory at the Battle of Cowpens, South Carolina, on January 17.

**1781**

In the last battle of the Revolutionary War, the British surrender at Yorktown, Virginia, on October 19.

**1783**

The Treaty of Paris, ending the Revolutionary War, is signed on September 3.

## REVOLUTIONARY WAR BATTLES, 1775–1781

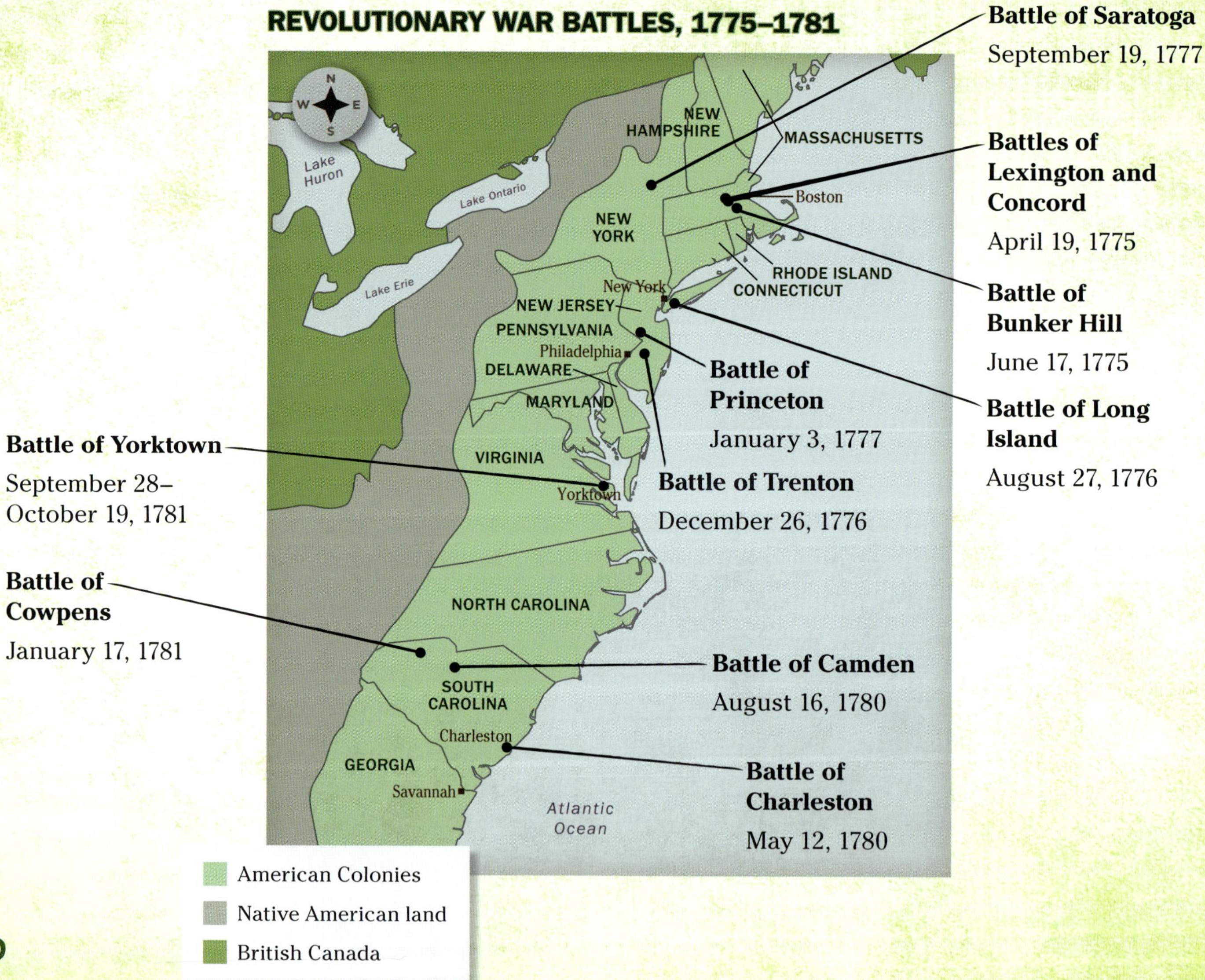

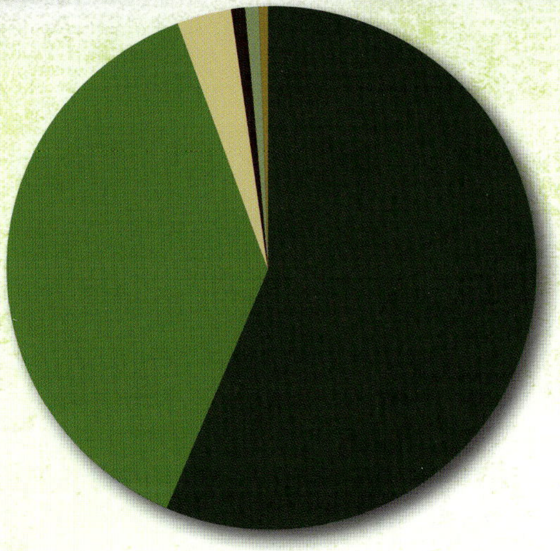

## CASUALTIES

**Total American Casualties: 10,623**

- Army deaths: 4,044
- Navy deaths: 342
- Marines deaths: 49
- Army wounded: 6,004
- Navy wounded: 114
- Marines wounded: 70

## KEY PLAYERS

**Benjamin Franklin** played an important role in securing French support for the Americans, which helped turn the tide of the war. Later, he was one of the American representatives who negotiated the Treaty of Paris with the British.

**General George Washington** led the Continental army and was later elected as the first president of the newly formed United States.

**General William Howe** was one of the generals who led the British army during the Revolutionary War. He defeated the Continental army at several battles, including the Battle of Brandywine and the Battle of Saratoga.

**King George III** was the British king who, along with Parliament, levied unpopular taxes against the American colonists.

**Marquis de Lafayette** was a young, wealthy Frenchmen who joined the patriots' cause. He was a brilliant military leader and helped convince the French government to support the Americans.

**artillery**
Large weapons used to fire long-range explosives.

**barrack**
A building used to house soldiers.

**bayonet**
A steel blade at the end of a rifle, used in hand-to-hand combat.

**casualty**
A death or injury suffered by a soldier in war.

**confiscate**
To seize or take by force.

**efficacious**
Effective or successful.

**infantry**
Soldiers trained to fight on foot.

**intelligence**
Information gathered about a rival or enemy.

**militia**

Citizen soldiers who fight locally and bring their own weapons and supplies with them into battle, typically returning home once a particular conflict has ended.

**musket**

A long, front-end-loaded gun, carried by infantry troops from the late 1500s through the mid-1800s.

**reconcile**

To make peace or to settle differences.

**regiment**

A military unit made up of several groups of troops.

**skirmish**

A small battle or clash.

**stalemate**

A draw.

## SELECTED BIBLIOGRAPHY

Chadwick, Bruce. *The First American Army: The Untold Story of George Washington and the Men behind America's First Fight for Freedom.* Naperville, IL: Sourcebooks, 2005. Print.

Savas, Theodore P., and J. David Dameron. *A Guide to Battles in the American Revolution.* El Dorado Hills, CA: Savas Beatie, 2010. Print.

Schecter, Barnet. *The Battle for New York: The City at the Heart of the American Revolution.* New York: Walker, 2002. Print.

## FURTHER READINGS

Earl, Sari. *George Washington: Revolutionary Leader & Founding Father.* Edina, MN: ABDO, 2010. Print.

Metz, Elizabeth Ryan. *I Was a Teenager in the American Revolution: 21 Young Patriots and Two Tories Tell Their Stories.* Jefferson, NC: McFarland, 2006. Print.

## WEB SITES

To learn more about the Revolutionary War, visit ABDO Publishing Company online at **www.abdopublishing.com**. Web sites about the Revolutionary War are featured on our Book Links page. These links are routinely monitored and updated to provide the most current information available.

## PLACES TO VISIT

### Cowpens National Battlefield

4001 Chesnee Highway
Gaffney, SC 29341
864-461-2828
http://www.nps.gov/cowp/index.htm
This is the site of one of the most important battles that took place in the South during the Revolutionary War.

### Independence Hall

143 South Third Street
Philadelphia, PA 19106
215-965-2305
http://www.nps.gov/inde/index.htm
This is one of the nation's most historic Revolutionary War buildings. Independence Hall is where the Second Continental Congress met, George Washington was appointed commander in chief, the Declaration of Independence was adopted, and the US Constitution was drafted.

### Valley Forge National Historical Park

1400 North Outer Line Drive
King of Prussia, PA 19406
610-783-1074
http://www.nps.gov/vafo/index.htm
This is where General George Washington and his men spent the bitter winter of 1777 to 1778.

## CHAPTER 1. A MUCH-NEEDED VICTORY

1. "Oct 17, 1777: Patriot Victory at Saratoga." *This Day in History.* A&E Television Networks, 2013. Web. 26 Feb. 2013.

2. "Hessians." *Liberty!: The American Revolution.* Twin Cities Public Television, 2004. Web. 25 Feb. 2013.

3. Richard Ketchum, ed. *The American Heritage Book of the Revolution.* New York: American Heritage, 1958. Print. 253.

4. Barnet Schecter. *The Battle for New York: The City at the Heart of the American Revolution.* New York: Walker, 2002. Print. 297.

## CHAPTER 2. COLONIAL UNREST

1. Tim Craig. "Obama to Use DC 'Taxation without Representation' License Plates." *Washington Post.* Washington Post, 15 Jan. 2013. Web. 25 Feb. 2013.

## CHAPTER 3. SHOTS FIRED

1. "Penelope Barker (1728–1796)." *National Women's History Museum.* NWHM, n.d. Web. 25 Feb. 2013.

2. Gerald A. Danzer, PhD, J. Jorge Klor de Alva, PhD, Louis E. Wilson, PhD, and Nancy Woloch, PhD. *The Americans.* Evanston, IL: McDougal Littell, 1998. Print. 98.

3. Ibid.

4. "Battles of Lexington and Concord." *History.* A&E Television Networks, 2013. Web. 26 Feb. 2013.

## CHAPTER 4. DECLARING INDEPENDENCE

1. David McCullough. *John Adams.* New York: Simon, 2001. Print. 95.

2. Gerald A. Danzer, PhD, J. Jorge Klor de Alva, PhD, Louis E. Wilson, PhD, and Nancy Woloch, PhD. *The Americans.* Evanston, IL: McDougal Littell, 1998. Print. 100.

3. Thomas Paine. *Common Sense.* New York: Peter Eckler, 1918. Print. 49.

4. Gerald A. Danzer, PhD, J. Jorge Klor de Alva, PhD, Louis E. Wilson, PhD, and Nancy Woloch, PhD. *The Americans.* Evanston, IL: McDougal Littell, 1998. Print. 100.

## CHAPTER 5. EARLY STRUGGLES

1. Barnet Schecter. *The Battle for New York: The City at the Heart of the American Revolution*. New York: Walker, 2002. Print. 99.

2. Phillip Papas. *That Ever Loyal Island: Staten Island and the American Revolution*. New York: New York UP, 2007. Print. 64.

3. Gerald A. Danzer, PhD, J. Jorge Klor de Alva, PhD, Louis E. Wilson, PhD, and Nancy Woloch, PhD. *The Americans*. Evanston, IL: McDougal Littell, 1998. Print. 107.

4. David McCullough. *1776*. New York: Simon, 2005. Print. 145.

5. Theodore P. Savas and J. David Dameron. *A Guide to Battles in the American Revolution*. El Dorado Hills, CA: Savas Beatie, 2010. Print. 55.

6. Ibid.

7. Ibid. 59.

8. "Patriot Nathan Hale Was Hanged September 22, 1776." *America's Story from America's Library*. Library of Congress, n.d. Web. 25 Feb. 2013.

9. Barnet Schecter. *The Battle for New York: The City at the Heart of the American Revolution*. New York: Walker, 2002. Print. 161.

## CHAPTER 6. A STIRRING COMEBACK

1. Barnet Schecter. *The Battle for New York: The City at the Heart of the American Revolution*. New York: Walker, 2002. Print. 266.

2. Theodore P. Savas and J. David Dameron. *A Guide to Battles in the American Revolution*. El Dorado Hills, CA: Savas Beatie, 2010. Print. 81.

3. "Battles of Trenton and Princeton." *History*. A&E Television Networks, 2013. Web. 26 Feb. 2013.

4. Barnet Schecter. *The Battle for New York: The City at the Heart of the American Revolution*. New York: Walker, 2002. Print. 267.

## CHAPTER 7. THE WAR RAGES ON

1. "History of the Battle of the Brandywine." *UShistory.org*. Independence Hall Association, 2013. Web. 27 Dec. 2012.

2. "History and Culture." *Valley Forge: National History Park, Pennsylvania*. National Park Service, 2013. Web. 26 Feb. 2013.

3. “Valley Forge FAQs.” *UShistory.org*. Independence Hall Association, 2013. Web. 27 Dec. 2012.

## CHAPTER 8. CHANGING STRATEGY

1. “The Battle of Monmouth 1778.” *BritishBattles.com*. BritishBattles.com, 2012. Web. 26 Feb. 2013.

2. Barnet Schecter. *The Battle for New York: The City at the Heart of the American Revolution*. New York: Walker, 2002. Print. 308.

3. “The Battle of Monmouth 1778.” *BritishBattles.com*. BritishBattles.com, 2012. Web. 26 Feb. 2013.

4. “Dec 29, 1778: British Capture Savannah, Georgia.” *This Day in History*. A&E Television Networks, 2013. Web. 26 Feb. 2013.

5. Ibid.

6. “May 12, 1780: Americans Suffer Worst Defeat of Revolution at Charleston.” *This Day in History*. A&E Television Networks, 2013. Web. 26 Feb. 2013.

7. “Aug 16, 1780: Continentals Routed at Camden, South Carolina.” *This Day in History*. A&E Television Networks, 2013. Web. 26 Feb. 2013.

8. John C. Dam, ed. *The Revolution Remembered: Eyewitness Accounts of the War for Independence*. Chicago: U of Chicago P, 1980. Print. 194–195.

9. “History and Culture.” *Guilford Courthouse National Military Park North Carolina*. National Park Service, 2012. Web. 26 Feb. 2013.

## CHAPTER 9. VICTORY AND PEACE

1. Francis D. Cogliano. *Revolutionary America, 1763–1815: A Political History*. New York: Routledge, 2008. Print. 110.

2. Ibid.

3. Sir Henry Clinton. “To Lord George Germain.” *Gentleman’s Magazine and Historical Chronicle* Volume 52 (1782): 8. Print. Albany, New York, 9–10, 12–15.

## ABOUT THE AUTHOR

Robert Grayson is an award-winning former daily newspaper reporter and the author of books for young adults. Throughout his journalism career, Grayson has written stories on historic events, sports figures, arts and entertainment, business, and pets, which have appeared in national and regional publications, including the *New York Yankees* magazine and *NBA Hoop*. He has written books about the Industrial Revolution, the California Gold Rush, animals in the military, and animal performers as well as the environment, law enforcement, and professional sports.